Third Word

Lyrics for the League of Intergalactic Hobos

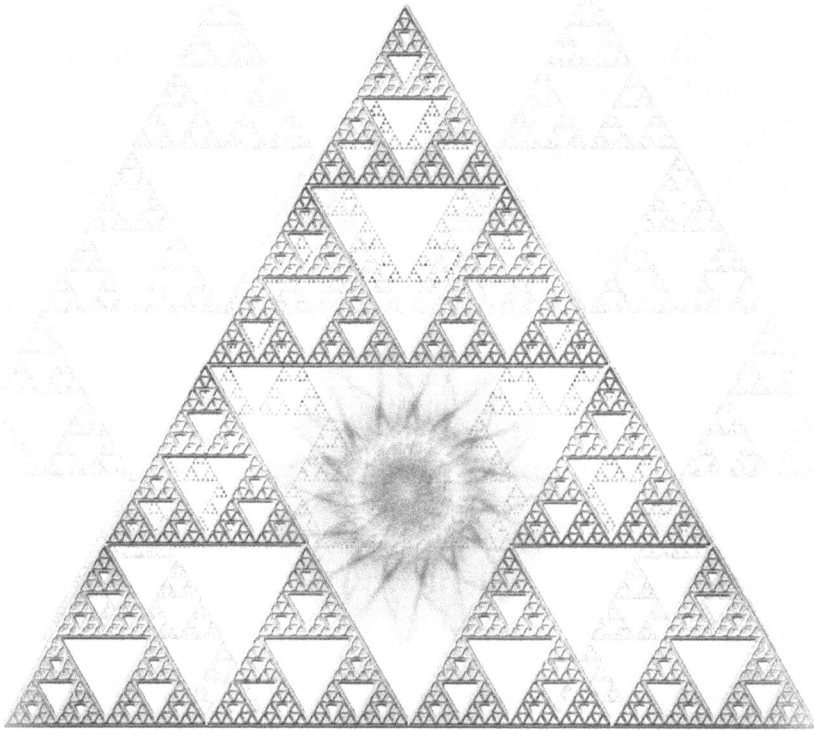

Indi Riverflow

Third Word
Triple Entendre
Indi Riverflow

ISBN-13: 978-0692416211
ISBN-10: 0692416218
©2015 Amana Mission Publishing Ink Alternative Press

Layout, design and images by:
Amana Mission All-In-One Media Magician

If you would like to adapt any lyric within this volume for musical composition or reprint, please contact us online: ***ampi@amanamission.com***

More writing from Indi Riverflow abounds
*Please visit **www.amanamission.com** to stay current*

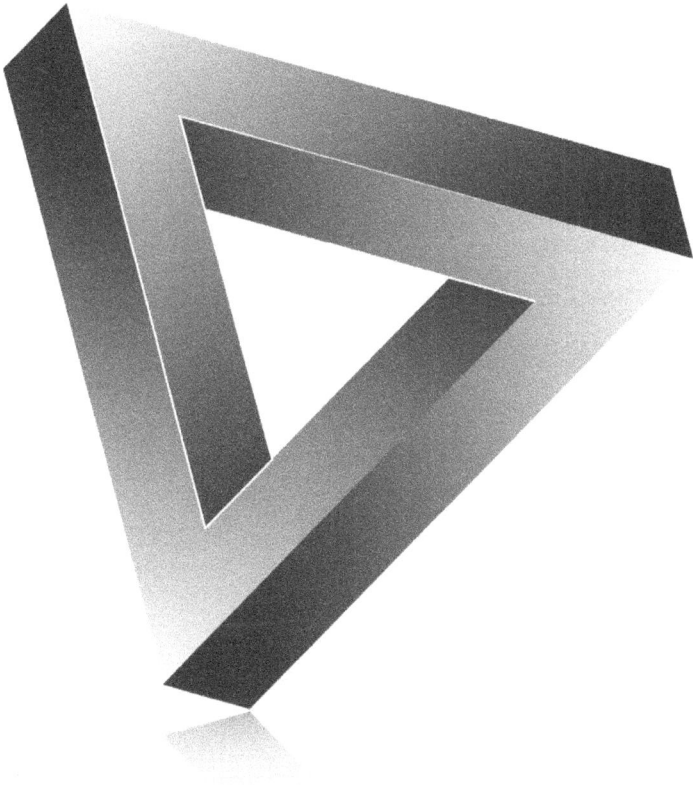

Amana Mission Publishing Ink
Alternative Press

To Incite Insight

Table of Context

Initiation

Start and start and start over again
Take a deep breath and count from ten
Ten powder-kegs of dynamite ignite
Nine novas erupt in the night
Eight awakenings crackle in dawn
Seven Sybils speak and then they are gone

Having a following
Doesn't mean you're a great leader
Like living in a library
Doesn't make you a great reader
There are no experts here
We're all beginners

Start and start and start over again
I don't even know where to begin
First was a burst of wild insight
Into intuition and off into flight
Next was a nexus of all time and space
Where I stared at the sky and saw my own face

Start and start and start over again
Trace time back through its origin
It began, it began, oh I lost count
But very long ago by all accounts
Everything happens but who knows when
So start and start and start over again

Having a following
Doesn't mean you're a great leader
Like living in a library
Doesn't make you a great reader
There are no experts here
We're all beginners

Start and start and start again
For we're still in initiation
On the wings of incantations
For dreams in generation
Spring-loaded cobras ready to dance
With any who dare to take the chance

Start and start and start over again
Pretty soon here we'll reach the end
All my mentors and tormentors
On the edge and near the center
We meet this moment here together
And start again forever and ever

Having a following
Doesn't mean you're a great leader
Like living in a library
Doesn't make you a great reader
There are no experts here
We're all beginners

Hotel Paradox

Right at the corner of Vortex Street
And Enigma Avenue
Squatters blew up the Utopia Suite
So we're booked in room Catch-22
Now is tomorrow with a twist
And you'd better believe nothing unreal exists

Oh, I swear we're halfway there
Down roundabout halls and endless stairs
Got to think around the box
To navigate this place
No vacancy in the Hotel Paradox
But we never run out of space
And we're halfway there
Always halfway
Halfway there

The front desk has already checked out
The pool full of atmosphere
The marquee is powered by doubt
'Cause if you knew, you wouldn't be here
If you have to ask, the answer is know
'Cause we ran out of answers ages ago

Oh, I swear we're halfway there
Down roundabout halls and endless stairs
Got to think around the box
To navigate this place
No vacancy in the Hotel Paradox
But we never run out of space
And we're halfway there
Always halfway
Halfway there

The time has come, the walrus said
To vacuum the upstairs ceiling
Time to lie in an unmade bed
And watch the paint a-peelin'
Well, nobody asked if you wanted to be
So free will's an illusion if you ask me

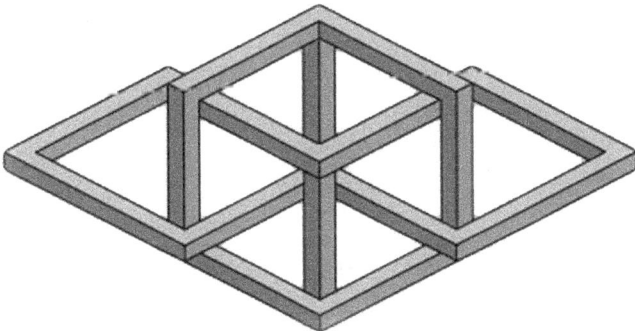

Every Third Word

Ouroboros before us
Ouroboros behind
In endless genesis
As the real unwinds

Eleven flying elevators
Eleventh hour chimes
It's forever now or never
A watch in rivers of time

We've heard rumors of humor
We've heard hints of absurd
And after the laughter
Grasp about every third word

Here in our hypersphere
Here under subterranean seas
Surging energetic vectors
Converging on you and me

Just us in juxtaposition
Just the wake of a dream
Wrap sounds around recursion
In surreal slipstreams

We've heard rumors of humor
We've heard hints of absurd
And after the laughter
Grasp about every third word

Double-twist contortionists
Double-takes and deja vu
Call me a hopeless optimist
A miracle's long overdue

Ouroboros before us
Ouroboros behind
In endless genesis
As the real unwinds

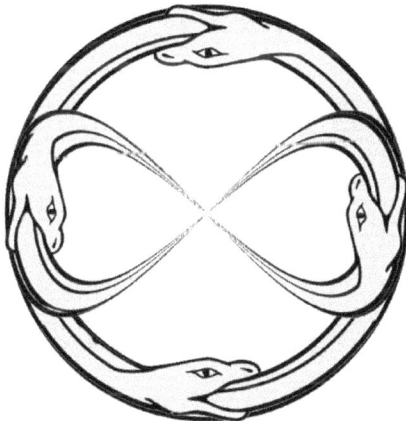

Velvet Valley

Going down to the velvet valley
Where syrup streams come to swell
Going down to tickle my fancy
And to tickle yours as well

Diving deep in quivering caverns
Imbibing the nexus of ecstasy
Sugar-soaked flooded cisterns
Overflowing with fantasies

The secret of Nature
It's on the tip of my tongue
It's on the tip of my tongue
It's on the tip of my tongue

Going down to the velvet valley
And I'm off to ring that belle
The kind that chimes luxuriously
Coaxing nectar from the well

Sipping milk of paradise
At the mouth of the sacred river
I weave a circle 'round her thrice
So she knows I come a giver

The secret of Nature
It's on the tip of my tongue
It's on the tip of my tongue
It's on the tip of my tongue

Going down to the velvet valley
That's where I'd rather dwell
Drinking all day that lovely honey
That renders one royal for a spell

Peeling back cloaked veils
Epicenter trembles and quakes
The breeze barely dares exhale
As the velvet valley shakes

The secret of Nature
It's on the tip of my tongue
It's on the tip of my tongue
It's on the tip of my tongue

Bloomin' Craft

Starseed from wild yonder frontier
Efflorescent effigies made of mirrors
Under the deep blue atmosphere
Sprouting at the bottom of an ocean of air

Overtures and undertones
Animating flesh and bone
Chipping away at the great unknown
As both the sculptor and the stone

A rose arose
With mistletoe arrows
Shooting from the shaft
Practicing the bloomin' craft

They carried carbon contraband
Written in twin helix strands
And it spread throughout the land
Like a red-hot firebrand

She showed them the invisible
She told them the inaudible
She described the ineffable
And bid them build the impossible

A rose arose
With mistletoe arrows
Shooting from the shaft
Practicing the bloomin' craft

Let's tend gardens of ornaments
Water our flowers in the darkness
If there are any unmixed sentiments
Left in the parched soil beneath us

She wished us illumination
But bid us bide among the blind
She whispered our initiation
By the sign of serpents intertwined

Chimera

'Twas the battle of White Mountain
Bohemian dreams in flames
And among the abandoned banners
Lay the opposites that were the same
Arsenals of vitriol
Launched in fits of ire
Save your face or save your soul
But either way it ends in fire

Chimera in a china shop
Bless the mess
It never stops
Ten thousand steps
To reach the top
But only one slip
For the bottom to drop

The clash of the sky Armadas
Under a musing moon
Eloquent wax melting
Janus candles lit too soon
Pyrite pyramids tower
As rockets burst above
Shooting stars don't go that far
When the wish runs out of love

Chimera in a china shop
Bless the mess
It never stops
Ten thousand steps
To reach the top
But only one slip
For the bottom to drop

There were jars of bottled lightening
Scorched Earth all around
Shards of shattered rainbows
Snowflakes rising from the ground
Assassinated characters
Faces full of sand
Low-down spilled across the hill
Casting shadows on the land

Spotlight Shadow

When the highway hum is overrun
And centuries handiwork undone
Drowned out by giant dragonflies
When the end of days draws nigh
And velvet darkness envelops the sky
Let's launch some fireworks before we die
While the grinning moon smiles wide
Look at you looking on the bright side

Under a spotlight
You know there's some shadows
Make it too bright
You'll blow off my halo
Say, my tale's airtight
Just killing time at Calypso's

When deck chairs are heaped in a pile
And the nearest land's ten thousand miles
The journey's taken a turn for the worse
And we've reached the outskirts of the universe
Somewhere out there the cyclone subsides
On castaways stranded without a guide
As broken violins roll in on the tide
Oh look at you looking on the bright side

Under a spotlight
You know there's some shadows
Make it too bright
You'll blow off my halo
Say, my tale's airtight
Just killing time at Calypso's

When all the alarms are on full blast
Fresh air scarce and vacuum vast
Tractor beams stream from the past
Molding today in yesterday's cast
Molecules multiply as atoms divide
Oceans flood as deserts are dried
Transparency has nowhere to hide
But look at you looking on the bright side

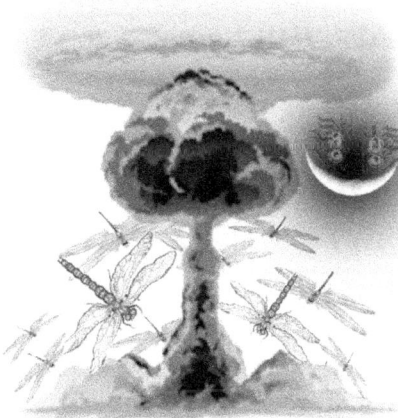

Pulling Strings

We met in booking at the local clink
Making the best of the situation
I'd had a little bit too much to think
Sparking a three-state investigation

She was in for numerous sins
And countless deviations
She flashed me an unlawful grin
The kind that needs no explanation

Oh, that good old outlaw romance
Sweatin' heavy and takin' our chance
Oh, you know, it's a dangerous dance
By the seat of our pants
Sometimes it comes apart at the seams
Whenever you start pulling strings
It might just keep unravelling

It was love at first mug shot
So I hurried back with her bail
And when they wouldn't let her out
I took down the walls of that damned jail

We ran off to join the circus
That scene was really fly-by-night
Swinging the high trapeze net-less
With backpacks of dynamite

Oh, that good old outlaw romance
Sweatin' heavy and takin' our chance
Oh, you know, it's a dangerous dance
By the seat of our pants
Sometimes it comes apart at the seams
Whenever you start pulling strings
It might just keep unravelling

One day the big top blew sky high
And we were already making tracks
Skating on thin ice of alibis
With the heat always at our backs

Never met a rule that wouldn't bend
We're completely self-authorized
I haven't a clue how all of this ends
But I plan on being surprised

Spice Caravan

Build your Byzantine
Opposite the blind
Rock the moat, stir up a scene
That'll really stick in their minds

We've got exotic concoctions
All-in-one remedies
Flagons of powerful potions
To mix up how you see

Grab some buckets
Line up your duckets
And drop your plans
It's catch as catch can
This spice caravan
Only rolls through here
Three quick trips a year

We've got arabesque mandalas
Piled crates of lucky charms
Enough powdered horns of dilemma
To fill ten thousand arms

There's a savvy vendor
Catering to any possible vice
And, man if you're a big spender
It's yours at twice the price

We stock every luxury
Of which you've never heard
Relics of forgotten dynasties
And guaranteed enchanted words

Grab some buckets
Line up your duckets
And drop your plans
It's catch as catch can
This spice caravan
Only rolls through here
Three quick trips a year

Fine merchants and magi
On dervish-laden bandwagons
An endless supply of stimuli
Too enticing to abandon

Over here is a sightless seer
Clad in invisible robes
If you come near he'll bend your ear
And twist your frontal lobe

Tripwire

Fire in the wax museum
Effigies melting down
But the fever's just a symptom
Of what's ailing this town

The fountain's spoutin' oil
The mountain's slick with grease
The river's fixin' to boil
And the valley knows no peace

Tracing the tripwire
Back to the trap
It sings like a siren
And stings like a slap
Oh, now I get the joke
Should have caught it before
How eloquently silence spoke
No need to wonder anymore

All alone with this megaphone
And hardly any ears to hear
Pluckin' feathers and pickin' bones
From the goose we cooked last year

No one knows the hour
Darkness caught us off guard
The bell has struck the tower
And the ground is shiftin' hard

Tracing the tripwire
Back to the trap
It sings like a siren
And stings like a slap
Oh, now I get the joke
Should have caught it before
How eloquently silence spoke
No need to wonder anymore

It's as if we've never met
Trading low-blow epithets
I only knew your silhouette
And we stand off as strangers yet

We're caricatures of who we were
Lobbing paint-filled grenades
Gone nuclear in the rear-view mirror
And precious little shade

Egg Drop

You'd never guess it from their tattered jackets
Four shadows sharing the glare
How they rode skyward chariots
And vaulted the moon on a dare
Well, I tell you, it was a sordid affair
How the clown confronted the crown
And both of their heads came tumbling down

Bubbles can't be unpopped
Eggs can't be undropped
And entropy can't be stopped
That's something Humpty Dumpty
Knew all too well
Hatching only happens
From the inside of the shell

So many variables to be shamboozled by
You'd never know it from the grit of the nitty
You'd never guess from the thick of the thin
All the worn-out grandeur and grime
Serving both shallow and sublime
Platinum-plated platitudes adorning our ears
Vying to be the ones that live on through the years

Bubbles can't be unpopped
Eggs can't be undropped
And entropy can't be stopped
That's something Humpty Dumpty
Knew all too well
Hatching only happens
From the inside of the shell

You'd never know it from their signs and seals
Dilated eyes and visionary zeal
Spaced-out trails and quantum tangles
Loose use of phrases and estimated angles
Meandering tales where the point evaporates
You'd never know they haunted the underworld
And crashed the pearly gates

Is it the glint or the glimmer you follow?
Is it the voice or the silence you heed?
Where do I sign up for a leader
Who leads me and leaves me to lead?
Yeah you might have thought otherwise
If they told you they had even a clue
Of what I'm telling, what I'm telling to you
Never mind the teller, it's the telling that's true

Eleventeen Reasons

What sacred cows shall we roast today?
Feeling completely absurd and a little risqué
Nay-sayers please stay out of the way
We're pulling off the impossible anyway

This world's just your mind inside-out
Converting a certain suspension of doubt
And I weary of always hearing about
The eleventeen reasons it'll never work out

Oh, that's me, I'm a four-panel cartoon
Carried away in a hot-air balloon
Y'all be singin' a different tune
When I'm mining diamonds all over the moon

What misguided missiles of hostility
Flaming in amazing futility
Sometimes your punchlines are partly funny
An easy left jab at truth's underbelly

Humor is more a mood than a sense
Dig all you want, I won't take offense
I'm happy to laugh at my own expense
It's a bargain at half the pretense

More than the sum of what I represent
In some random scheme of connected events
Classified as a bona fide quadruple agent
But I can't say by whom or what I was sent

Oh, that's me, I'm a four-panel cartoon
Carried away in a hot-air balloon
Y'all be singin' a different tune
When I'm mining diamonds all over the moon

Perfectly Dodecahedral

The bellwether whistles
At the crack of noon
No, don't you lounge on your laurels
Destiny called and she'll be here soon

Better sprinkle a little ink on the canvas
And spread my head out on the floor
She ought to get a kick out of this
Number one hundred forty-four
When she knocks just open the door
Like a dozen dozen times before

How shall I number thee?
Let me count the ways
Phrases pop out of the strangest places
Like a foghorn in the haze
And the coffee cups keep piling up
Just like the yesterdays
Waiting for the mountain to erupt
And taking on a tint of gray

This one's special
It's a twelve by twelve vessel
A signature time capsule
Engine hyper-dimensional
With a triple quad transaxle
Perfectly dodecahedral

They are so numbered on Olympus
And in the Bible's tribes
They are the labors of Hercules
And the clock of Zodiac signs
They are the conduits of signals
Entering the house of the mind

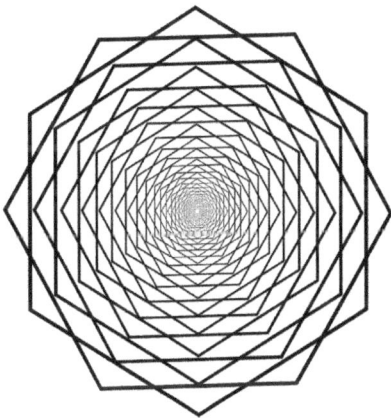

High John

Oh, no, Low John done done it again
Made off with the boss' favorite pen
And wrote a note that said it all
Nailed it up on the parlor wall

By the power divested of me
Every one of you is free
Consider it a royal decree
I declare a state of liberty

Oh, no, boss man, we won't work no more
You bought yourself more than you bargained for
Whips just make me whistle Dixie down
And the hounds come 'round to bay with the sound

Let the cotton go rotten
The Devil can have this plantation
In case you've forgotten
I was born the prince of a nation

I'm faster than that whip-cracking bastard
And that's what makes the real master
Curse of the conquered can be slow, slow poison
Takes centuries to sink in
Under your children's children's skin

They'll shuffle to jungle rhythms
They'll howl at the moon
They'll weigh out their freedom
By the mile and the tune
They'll abandon your kingdoms
And sleep in till noon

Oh, no, boss man, we won't work no more
You bought yourself more than you bargained for
Whips just make me whistle Dixie down
And the hounds come 'round to bay with the sound

Cultivating mutiny under your boot
The unquiet is silent but is not mute
And every agitator you shoot
Summons a dozen more in tribute
When you come face to face with your fruit
You'll see in what a swamp you settled your roots

Don't y'know, little Pharaoh
Anyone can swing the king's lingo
They call me High John or John the Low
And I don't kiss any man's toe
You can take your status quo
And stick it where the sun don't glow

Butterfly Effect

Some see marble and others a chisel
And some see a monumental deed
I see you can count the seeds in an apple
But who can count the apples in a seed?

Nostradamus always stuck to his story
But he was careful with his wagers
Missing the mark never made him worry
It all shakes loose sooner or later

Let's play a game of pin the tale
Pin the tale on the circuit tree
Many levels and steps to scale
Devil hides in the fine details
Fractal forms forever branching
Read tea leaves, Tarot or I Ching
Whichever way you swing
Everything shifts with a butterfly wing

Three-ringed psychokinetic circus
Uncanny leaps of synchronicity
With all these signs between us
It's a wonder anyone can see

You might write it off to happenstance
An offbeat quirk of circumstance
A meaningless coincidence
Just an act of random chance

Let's play a game of pin the tale
Pin the tale on the circuit tree
Many levels and steps to scale
Devil hides in the fine details
Fractal forms forever branching
Read tea leaves, Tarot or I Ching
Whichever way you swing
Everything shifts with a butterfly wing

One could say it was all foreordained
Part of some vast cosmic plan
Or just a way to keep us entertained
Seering in the frying pan

Then the dots connect themselves
In constellations unforeseen
Whatever Fate's ulterior motives
For making such a scene

Sugar-Coated Half-Truths

I'm not trying to run for sainthood
Nor vying for a Nobel prize
I plan to be good and misunderstood
Accidentally canonized

My miracles are mighty meager
Y'all better bring your own wine
Yes, I've been known to walk on water
But only in the winter time

Sugar-coated half-truths
Go better with a shaker of salt
And if you wind up in Heaven
It ain't gonna be my fault
You can thank yourself later
Do us both a favor
And be your own savior

Wouldn't be caught dead in chain-mail
No, knighthood is not for me
Not on a hunt for some bloody Grail
And I say leave the dragons be

I harbor no political ambitions
You won't see me on campaign signs
The After-Party is my affiliation
And if nominated I'll decline

Sugar-coated half-truths
Go better with a shaker of salt
And if you wind up in Heaven
It ain't gonna be my fault
You can thank yourself later
Do us both a favor
And be your own savior

Oh I'll serve my head on a platter
If that's what the Muses crave
For the love of what truly matters
Carried away in the carrier waves

Just a Mariachi for your courtships
Playing in this moment you designed
Songs on my lips as I'm gathering tips
And leaving a little peace on my mind

Tempest In A Teacup

When I said let them eat cake I didn't mean mine
Can't eat the cake and have it served with wine
Oh, that gallows humor straightens the spine
But if the set-up is strung with six feet of twine
Who's hanging around for the punchline?

They said that Dante wrote comedies
But they didn't seem all that funny to me
Who hasn't laughed at pratfall tragedy
Removed from proximity
When the scenario's fit for parody
Humor's just a matter of degree

What's the trouble?
Another kerfuffle
Oh, no, somebody burst a bubble
We'll light a candle
For the latest struggle

You know I have no use for enemies
Even less for friends like these
That ten heavens wouldn't please
Unless Hell would also freeze
This petty air makes me sneeze
Setting off all sorts of allergies

It's a tempest in a teacup
And the kettle is burning up
Screaming it's the pot that's hot
And the fire's in on the plot
Turning downsides to upshots
Takes more patience than I've got
We're all less than impressed
So let's do our best to give it a rest

Oh, it's an errand fit for a Fool
Making waves in shallow pools
Starting starships with lighter fuel
Numb to rumbles of ridicule
Under the hot button but staying cool
Cause this moment is miniscule

What's the trouble?
Another kerfuffle
Oh no, somebody burst a bubble
We'll light a candle
For the latest struggle

Gonzo Bonkers

Round peg, square slot
It's a familiar routine
Then they break out the inkblots
And ask you what they mean

But they don't know, no
Anymore than you or I do
It's true, they haven't a clue
What those pictures look like to you

Entertain your visions in seclusion
They'll call it a raving mad delusion
Get enough kooks to join in
And suddenly it becomes a religion
It's a joke and we're the butts
Not being crazy would be a little nuts

I'm a tad mad batty
I must admit
Why deny it
If the straitjacket fits

It's always the oddballs
On the cusp of innovation
Maybe loosing your marbles
Is the secret of salvation

The difference between madness and genius
Seems to be about a generation
So give me twenty years, more or less
And you'll have your explanations

Oh, yeah, we've gone gonzo bonkers
The Coo-Coo done flew over
Ten miles off our rockers
And running rings around our keepers

Entertain your visions in seclusion
They'll call it a raving mad delusion
Get enough kooks to join in
And suddenly it becomes a religion
It's a joke and we're the butts
Not being crazy would be a little nuts

Meets the Eye

Crazy Bear said you gotta flip your lid
If you want to see the other side
Peer past the grids and pyramids
Where the pattern gets magnified
Magnified
And amplified
The sirens sigh
So much more than meets the eye

Oh crystal ball
Oh crystal ball
All cracked up at the oracle
Said always choose an alternative
And when in doubt, be decisive
I get the message clear and loud
Spelled out in shapeshifting clouds

I met her down at the nebula's edge
Plasma mandalas all around
She asked if I could spare some space
For we've run out of ground
Out of ground
We fell spellbound
In torus twine
So much more than meets the eye

We were on the same kind of vibe
Frequency freaks tuning in
Decided we must be two of a tribe
So we took our world out for a spin
For a spin
Wound up within
Spiral vortex skies
So much more than meets the eye

If you ever catch a glimpse of your destiny
Some hint of what might come
Stay away from free-lance prophecy
That game gets pretty zero-sum
Zero-sum
What it becomes
I see yours but not mine
So much more than meets the eye

History sure ain't what it used to be
Jaded and riddled with stray blasé
Today is living out a parody
The past getting so passé
So passé
It's gone away
Like yesterday's pie
But there's so much more than meets the eye

Fabric Meets the Flesh

Winter blew through and froze my bones
The angels throwing hailstones
We've crossed Juno, just so you know
And she's notching icicles in her crossbow

The best laid plans of men and mice
Left us highways paved with ice
Snowballs rolling big and bold
I hope that jack-shack's gonna hold

When the fabric meets the flesh
And the veils fall in soft caress
When art devours artifice
And we stand naked nonetheless

When the meta is consumed by meat
Theories are great, but when do we eat?
You can lead minds to the kitchen sink
But I don't believe you can make them think

Back to the old drawing board
See if this one strikes a chord
The blueprint's only paper-thin
When the human element enters in

When the fabric meets the flesh
And the veils fall in soft caress
When art devours artifice
And we stand naked nonetheless

If you'd plan to span the globe
Clad in royal threadbare robes
Well, every strength comes along
With weakness born of being strong

When ideas hit hard reality
Dragged by tractor-beams of gravity
And the parachute snags and tears
Remember we're always halfway there

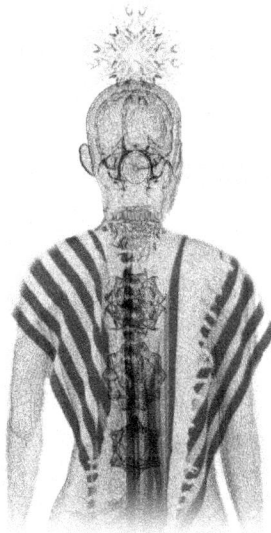

Monosyllable

Ninepence in the pocket
Muffin up a canoe
Stirring up the jampot
Dripping with honeydew

Scaling Venusian mountains
Turning a blind eye to sight
Awash in Cyprian fountains
Wading through jewel-boxes of delight

Well, they call it the Tropics
'Cause it's steamy hot and wet
And as far as a topic
That's as close as it gets

Climbing up the plum tree
Puddings in a ring
Sweeter than any candy
The confectioner might bring

Licking the night physic
Merging converging nerves
Frantic and spasmodic
Along hyperbolic curves

Well, they call it the Tropics
'Cause it's steamy hot and wet
And as far as a topic
That's as close as it gets

Trouble comes a-knocking
With a twisted mistletoe sprig
Double-backed beast bucking
In a furious Paphian jig

It's a venerable monosyllable
A veritable cascade
A source as inexhaustible
As the way we all were made

Alembic

The face of the tabula rasa
Blank slate awaiting the wind
Like the priestess of Pythia
Inhaling infinity within

Did you anticipate my arrival
Grasping wisps of worn coat-tails?
Can you taste the rag-tag sense of style
Can you hear the breeze rustling these sails?

Coaxed into a maelstrom
A thundering song for a stormy dawn
And here everybody comes
And there everyone has gone

Canvas stretched on rubber bands
Exotic ink fetched from faraway lands
Images etched in hourglass sands
Keep whatever you catch in your hands

I dreamt my way to this domain
Dancing into the serpent's lair
I came in the name of the goddess of grain
So blissfully unaware

At the crossroads the curtain rippled
Centuries swept away
And then our numbers were tripled
When the djinn came out to play

We've caught a drop of magic
Raining from phantom clouds
Distilled in the alembic
Until it sings the spell out loud

Canvas stretched on rubber bands
Exotic ink fetched from faraway lands
Images etched in hourglass sands
Keep whatever you catch in your hands

S.S. Rudderless

All you weirdos freaks and geeks
Outlaws living in hide and seek
Crushed orchids who fear to speak
And anyone else with a wild streak

Calling all agents of aberration
Welcome to phase eleven
Of our radical master plan
To achieve total global deviation

This is the S.S. Rudderless
It appears we're pretty leaderless
No one ever seems to bring a compass
And where we're headed is anyone's guess

Scruffy ruffians and rabble, rouse
All round pegs the square disavows
Oh ye of lofty and earthy brows
With more wit than the law allows

Astral adepts and mystic mavens
Carnival crews and gypsy ravens
Designers of slow-roll fascination
Restless jesters juggling connotation

This is the S.S. Rudderless
It appears we're pretty leaderless
No one ever seems to bring a compass
And where we're headed is anyone's guess

Clowns sporting technicolor crowns
All the movers and shakers of sound
Denizens of the underground
In for a penny down for a pound

Bards and bandits and spray-paint scribes
Bridge dwellers and roving tribes
Travelers who never appear to arrive
Just trying to keep the trip alive

Kaleidoscope Catalyst

Once upon a lovely summer dawn
A generation went boom
And many lines went undrawn
When the walls ran out of room
Splintered and cast adrift
Scattered by the technicolor shift
Oh, you can feel the aftershocks
From that rumbling quake
Like an avalanche of rolling rocks
That still makes foundations shake

Went to the Universe City
Where it's all matter of degree
Saw the walls breathing relativity
So I dropped out
Turned on
And tuned in
With a crystal clear batch of pure Phd

Liquid synchronicity dust
Problem child of a Swiss bicyclist
The kaleidoscope catalyst
Kaleidoscope catalyst

Man, the age was more than Aquarian
It was overtly subversive
And downright contrarian
When so many senses combined
Tasting synesthesia views
It blew a few minds
Knocked loose a few screws
Turned on cultures colorblind
To intangible magical hues

Liquid synchronicity dust
Problem child of a Swiss bicyclist
The kaleidoscope catalyst
Kaleidoscope catalyst

Oh yes that sound is still around
Though fainter with every year
But if you keep both ears to the ground
There's just enough left to hear
Lost secret dimensions
The rye's no mystery to me
For my essence is Eleusinian
Awaiting the return of Persephone

Faux Mirage

Never trust a psychic
Who requires appointments
If they were truly authentic
They'd have your slot pencilled in
I'm not calling anyone a charlatan
But this snake-oil seems mighty thin
Have you taste-tested your own medicine?

I once bought some free advice
The very best kind you can get
If they sell you your own soul at market price
That ain't enlightenment
No, that ain't enlightenment

We've come to some oasis
Where the water tastes like truth
Filtered by reverse osmosis
And delivered to the youth
For the thirsty do not inquire
If that cup of Kool-Aid is pure
When it quenches the heart's desire
And comforts the unsure

Volition is like a faux mirage
It feels real in the heat of the choice
Fate comes in camouflage
Imitating a stranger's voice
Even counterfeits have a certain charm
And if no one's the wiser
How does one find the harm?

Adorned with graven emblems
Covered in costume jewelry
Numb to the shiny conundrum
Embedded in star-struck marquees
No side trip is out of the way
When redemption's the destination
Every detour and every delay
Serve the cause of creation

I once bought some free advice
The very best kind you can get
If they sell you your own soul at market price
That ain't enlightenment
No, that ain't enlightenment

Gremlins On Theremins

Say, I hear you play air guitar
Like a million-dollar rockstar
Swinging that axe and looking sharp
But can you tease the untouchable harp
Gesture forth eerie arias
Worthy of unseen phantom operas
Conjure concertos from the ether
Waiting to be plucked out of thin air
Do you dare the instrument that isn't there?

Windows open on voices of wind
Stringless space
Tracing vapor's song
There's gremlins in the theremin
What could possibly go wrong?

And when you're all alone
In the chaos zone of the etherphone
Where shapes of sound are shown
To be simply composed of volume and tone
Surfing sonic waves of good vibrations
On marionette strings of energy
Naked hands singing melodies
Handled with flash and sorcery

Windows open on voices of wind
Stringless space
Tracing vapor's song
There's gremlins in the theremin
What could possibly go wrong?

Tuning the vast sonar ocean
To the tones of lunar emotions
Listening for that perfect explosion
Of constant variation
The will that trills notes so tender
Full of unsung songs to render
When the airborne corps all surrender
And the bombs are marked return to sender

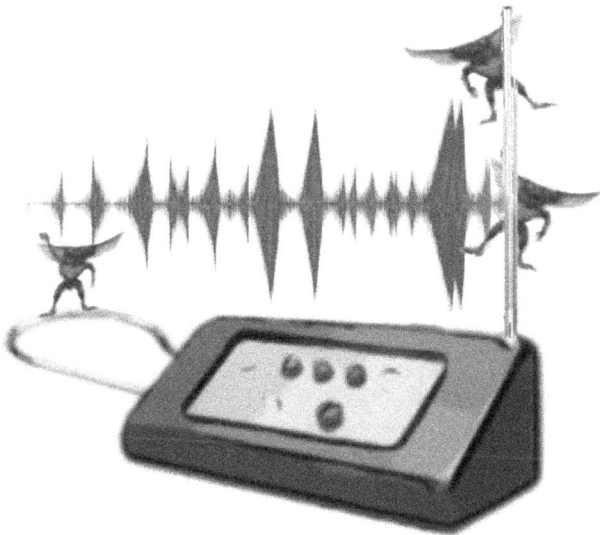

Ghost Writer Boogie

Takes a special kind of crazy
To host a ghost in stride
Ride you like a pale pookah
Down to the séance inside

The parlor's dark and smoky
Where we ouija the night away
Spirits tapping skeleton keys
Marked in spectral shades of grey

I'm a lunatic moonlighter
And it's another all-nighter
Head's in a blender
Phantoms on a bender
The night has never looked brighter
For the faithful ghost writer

Here great vats of ink are spilled
Symbols distilled into scripts
Pages of ages quilled and filled
From mosaic sealed crypts

Here our ears are turned to portals
Our eyes melt in pools of souls
Tuned to the channel of immortals
As the ferryman gathers his tolls

I'm a lunatic moonlighter
And it's another all-nighter
Head's in a blender
Phantoms on a bender
The night has never looked brighter
For the faithful ghost writer

We listen for ephemeral whispers
Voices in the rustling leaves
Trailing echoes in the vapor
Heirlooms weaving in the eves

It's a quest for the quintessential
In a quagmire of wasted designs
On a nova of untapped potential
Imagination dressed to the nines

Pivot Point

Pivot point, pivot point,
Which foot leads?
It's a chance dart
Tossed at a dance chart
Go back to what's left
Or right on at full speed
What you can't do is leave it up in the air
Pick a direction or you'll go nowhere

Pivot point, pivot point
It's a poignant choice
Down that hard rocky ground
Guts and glory bound
Or turn back around
And own your hometown
Retelling second-hand stories under a mask
Over and over to anyone who asks

Pivot point, pivot point
Who else can we appoint?
It's your land to expand
Head for new peaks
Or tread in quicksand
That's Excalibur in your hands
Man, swing that sword like it's your own
For you're the one that pulled it out of the stone

Pivot point, pivot point
Hopscotch for your life
Bending with trends
Leads to crowded dead-ends
Though many may attend
Bringing eager ears to lend
Tomorrow follows the course set now
There's no choosing when, only how

Pivot point, pivot point
Fate swivels on this juncture
Blast faster to the past
Or cast it off for the future
Craft tomorrow's architecture
Build something new to last
Or play forever under flags at half-mast
Whatever you do, don't hesitate
That drawbridge gate ain't fixin' to wait

Blues For Kali

They call Her the Dark Mother
And the Mountain's Daughter
She'll sever your head
And deliver up another
Matters may not get better
But they'll be different all the same
For that chatter don't matter
And the matter won't really mind
When you go to leave all the Maya behind

Each day is a tango with death
Dancing true blue tempos
Among shadows and echoes
Simple as holding a breath
And then letting it go
Jai Ma Kali Namo

She's the mistress of mystery
Far as any Third Eye can see
Her method is madness
And madness is mandatory
In order to shake off reality
Mortal plane's a crazy game
Just playing at being you and me
Takes grace to face a Kali makeover
But you'll get over whoever you were

Each day is a tango with death
Dancing true blue tempos
Among shadows and echoes
Simple as holding a breath
And then letting it go
Jai Ma Kali Namo

Recycling all forms of energy
The mighty queen of Kundalini
Tantamount to Tantra
The Universe's Yoni
We're transitory stories
Changing faces places and names
Kali Durga Uma Parvati
That which clings will surely be torn
Nothing to mourn, we're all Being reborn

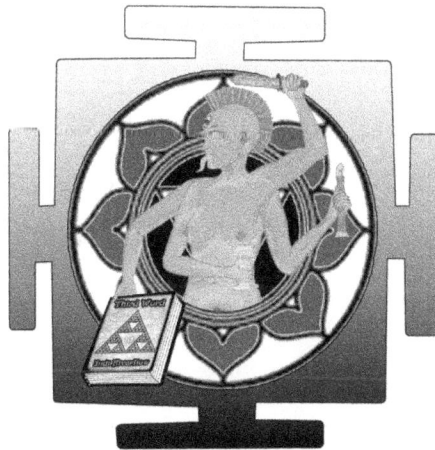

Noon

It's a Sphinx without a riddle
An oubliette without a hatch
A bow without a fiddle
Or a torch without a match

Noon
Now I won
Never odd or even
No, it is opposition
Drawn onward
Are we not drawn onward to a new era?
Drawn onward
No it is opposition
Never odd or even
Now I won
Noon

It's a coil without a center
An explosion with no force
A device with no inventor
Or a stream without a source

Ma is as selfless as I am
Mirror rim
So many dynamos
Pull up level pull up

Sifted through filters
Forward or backward
Spelled the same
The eternal eye
That became my name

Pull up level pull up
So many dynamos
Mirror rim
Ma is as selfless as I am

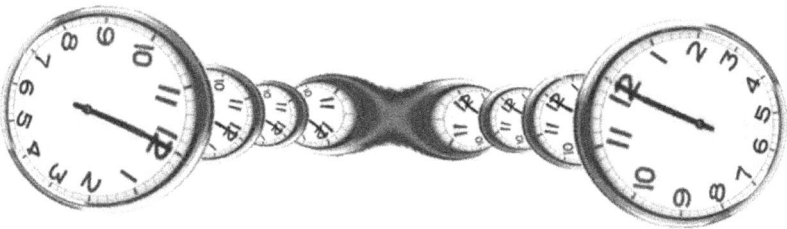

League of Intergalactic Hobos

Caught this hotfoot surfing volcanoes
But only when the lava tide's low
Touring Texarkana via tornado
Pursuing rumors of ice-blue buffalo
Hitched a northbound balloon 'n damn near froze
Selling kilos of snow to the Eskimos
Courting the worst-case scenario
With a chain-gang of leprechauns in tow
Oh, you have to know this ain't my first rodeo

Hopping from fiasco to fiasco
By freight train or UFO
Openly incognito
Not your usual superheroes
The League of Intergalactic Hobos

From Jupiter to Juneau
Those hobos stuck it to the status quo
Sowing turbo-boosted embryos
Row after row, seeds of indigo
On the fast track to tomorrow
Little exploding rainbows
Tuned to the new age pirate radio
The age-old show to end all shows
And we're all coming on for a cameo

Hopping from fiasco to fiasco
By freight train or UFO
Openly incognito
Not your usual superheroes
The League of Intergalactic Hobos

Hanging with vagabonds of voodoo
Inked with tattoos of Stygian blue
On a rendezvous to the usual snafus
At the basement of Twenty-Three Skidoo
Where new planes of existence debut
Some of you'd faint from the fumes of that brew
Truth you can't help but misconstrue
You get a sense that nothing is truly new
And that in the end you are what you do

Hopping from fiasco to fiasco
By freight train or UFO
Openly incognito
Not your usual superheroes
The League of Intergalactic Hobos

Saturn's Return

She was ravishing in rags
She banished gloom from the drag
Serving fantasies by the bag
Any mark would be taken in by the shine
Oh it's no use cryin' over spilt wine
And no use whining about wilted vines
Especially when the vineyard was never mine

She interrupted nothing, nothing at all
I was deeply contemplating the nearest wall
Innocently planning on procrastinating
My pre-wasted day away
But I lost sight of my priorities
And put the pause button on delay

Maybe it was her eyes, or maybe her ink
Maybe it was her fire or just my drink
Whatever it was that made me think
Kick-starting grinding gears in my head
Oh, I'll do nothing tomorrow instead

She liked to insert such terms
As hyperbolic tessellation
In the course of casual conversation
Dangling participles in anticipation
Of fruitless furtive flirtations
Daring you to confess incomprehension
Of notions which need no explanation

Classy and class-conscious all at once
She dropped out of finishing school
And jumped into the blue gene pool
Elitism isn't for everyone she said
The books kept slipping off my head
And anyway they'd rather be read

Maybe it was her eyes, or maybe her ink
Maybe it was her fire or just my drink
Whatever it was that made me think
Kick-starting grinding gears in my head
Oh, I'll do nothing tomorrow instead

She had a way of waxing eloquent
On any subject she'd care to invent
She was of roundly angular bent
And I was rarely sure exactly what she meant
She always assumed that you understood
I always assumed I eventually would

What a bundle of conflicted contradictions
A wonderful mess of conflated convictions
In a ribbon-red dress defying description
Surfing the wave of Saturn's Return
She had three triple lifetimes to burn
And so when she said shall we then go
And I said where and she said you know
She said you know, she said you know

Split In Two

Here I am your tragic hero
Kicking rocks down at ground zero
Oh, I feel a little bit like Nero
Fiddling while my village burns
But I really had to finish that solo
For whomever it may concern

Oh, I know I'm courting disaster
Hell, that's half the adventure
Until they cure human nature
I'm split in two loving both of you

When Eris asked young Paris
For what will you be embarrassed?
Is it power or wit or lady's love?
He chose the loveliest on Earth or above
And for that Troy did not last
And all of Lydia faded into the past

Now then and tomorrow
Playing tug of war with my soul
To the left the edge of a fifty-foot ledge
Plunging to piranha-filled fishbowls
On the right a wasteland of quicksand
Bordering on forests of smoldering coals

Oh, I know I'm courting disaster
Hell, that's half the adventure
Until they cure human nature
I'm split in two loving both of you

I never wanted to start a war
Oh no, that's not what love is for
But restless hearts aren't secure
And they always yearn for more
Love than sits in the reservoir

Skating the surface of frozen lakes
How much breaking can we take?
This ice is brittle thin and weak
It might shatter if I so much as speak
Fancy footwork gets swiftly undone
When the ground melts under the sun

It sucks at the center of the centrifuge
Rinsing off the subterfuge
Making my peace with old and new
Looks like the only thing to do
For I'm running out of refuge
And there's no delay to stay the deluge

Taste of Gnosis

Went to wish in a meteor shower
Fortune flashing in eventide
Splashing past for hours
As the atmosphere rarified
Spying specks of stellar powder
On a spectacular final slide
To collide with the blazing Tower
Arcing sparks of the starry-eyed

Seering bolts of wonder
Cracking wide the crown
You can try to race the thunder
But it's a long, long way down
You can try to race the thunder
But it's a long, long way down

Have we had a taste of Gnosis
Or sophisticated sophistry?
Acquiring by osmosis
Qualities of tangibility
Garden-path hypnosis
Parsing psychic circuitry
Granting form to amorphous
Extra-sensory imagery

Seering bolts of wonder
Cracking wide the crown
You can try to race the thunder
But it's a long, long way down
You can try to race the thunder
But it's a long, long way down

When the phoenix does arise
And the scorched Earth regrows
When emergence is self-catalyzed
Glowing in radial halos
Crackling like raging skies
Over Lake Maracaibo
Where the elements electrify
At the mouth of the Catatumbo

Golden Fleece

There's a reason they call it the Golden Fleece
All those Argonauts signed a release
Squeaky pulleys call for grease
So excuse me while I disturb some peace

Getting mixed signals from the Oracle
Hard to know if we're heroes or fools
From the cryptic tone of ridicule
Coming off that three-legged stool

The prize is priceless
And beggars belief
Guarded by a dragon
With warriors for teeth
I'd rest on my laurels
But they made off with my wreath
Plenty of glory in the age-old stories
Plenty of shadows underneath

All these luminaries merit mention
The hero is an epic invention
A way to focus dramatic tension
A plot device, a narrative convention

Forecast's sunny with dark undertones
And some details are best left unknown
You'll succeed through no fault of your own
If you can tell an island from a stepping-stone

The prize is priceless
And beggars belief
Guarded by a dragon
With warriors for teeth
I'd rest on my laurels
But they made off with my wreath
Plenty of glory in the age-old stories
Plenty of shadows underneath

Oh, I'm no stranger to galley stripes
Quite acquainted with all the archetypes
Whatever treasure a pirate may swipe
Is merely a measure of the wind in your pipes

Hell, we all gathered to tell the tale
And my tea leaves say this quest can't fail
Hunt your holy grails and your white whales
Just lend me some headwinds for my sails

Night-Sea Swimmer

As far as I can tell the world's all wet
And I'm paddling without an oar
Survival seems an unsafe bet
With odds so astronomically poor
Oh, you'll hear tall tales told of shore
But I've never met anyone yet
Who can say they've been there before

There's no point in going slow
Shakin' a tail and one shot to spend
Carrying blueprint codes to the motherlode
Chasing the glow at the tunnel's end
All swept up in the undertow
Billions of brothers and not one friend

Bursting forth at bullet pace
Night-sea swimmers in full chase
Only one winner takes this race
No future comes for second place

How could any being ever be so low?
I sure can't fathom who would throw
The lot of us thus into these dark seas
But somehow I know
He must be just like me

Jettisoned in unison
From a loaded silent cannon
Spilling by the billion
Into sightless lightless oceans
All with the singular motivation
Of landing an ovation

Bursting forth at bullet pace
Night-sea swimmers in full chase
Only one winner takes this race
No future comes for second place

The poor sots out there treading
Precious seconds shedding
Hey, if we don't get where we're heading
We're most surely bound to drown
And I don't see any lifeboats around

I don't know what awaits on Earth
On the other side they're calling birth
But I'm sure the universe will burst
If I don't manage to get there first

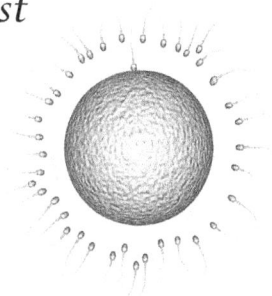

Painted Epiphanies
For Hunter

A word on the tongue is worth ten in the head
It'll never be heard if it never gets said
You know, a closed mouth never gets fed
Wind up with pie in the eye instead

Repeating history's all the rage
Most of the action goes down off-stage
Painted epiphanies faded with age
There's a flip side to every page

Toss a pebble
Unlock the rain
Gather your vessels
As the crescent moon wanes
Here comes a flood
Of tears sweat and blood
Washing out the shallow plain
Weep not for all that spills
Rejoice for what remains

There I go, waking dragons in their dens
Tickling unguarded abdomens
Ruffling feathers without raising a pen
Must've been speaking out loud again

Hatchets buried under tons of dirt
Just let it slide and no one gets hurt
This molehill's too deep to desert
And I'll be glad to get out with my shirt

Toss a pebble
Unlock the rain
Gather your vessels
As the crescent moon wanes
Here comes a flood
Of tears sweat and blood
Washing out the shallow plain
Weep not for all that spills
Rejoice for what remains

So serve the story that lives to be told
Never bought or sold, not for pale gold
That's the creed we're held to uphold
Casting plaster in a hunter's mold

We're surely checked into the Mission
A sweet and melancholy tradition
Set on a course in matter transmission
I'll count myself rich if I've paid my tuition

The Pattern
A shadow of Amber

When you set out to tread the Pattern
Past and future fuse
Upswings and downturns
Follow the frequency of clues
You'll remember more than you ever forgot
And relearn more you might ever be taught

Like walking through a brick wall
Once you start you'd better not stall
Gonna get there if I have to crawl
All those barriers and obstacles
They were the path after all

When you build momentum
Opposites grow exact
Whirling around fulcrums
Made of what the other lacked
Rising and falling in alternate slots
Drawing definition from all you are not

When the walker and Pattern merge
And millennia melt
An animal of pure survival urge
Where the spark of life itself
Seeks the void and ultimate relief
From the terminal grind of outlining motifs

Like walking through a brick wall
Once you start you'd better not stall
Gonna get there if I have to crawl
All those barriers and obstacles
They were the path after all

Each step casts emanations
Resonating throughout the planes
Spawning unknown imitations
Who pump water through their veins
It's a myriad mirror applying Order
To the Chaotic madness at the heart of Amber

And if you run into my shadow
You'll know I went the other way
In a direction none may follow
Where ten years pass here in but a day
By the horn of the Unicorn shall verity ring
Rhythm-driven Random was always the King

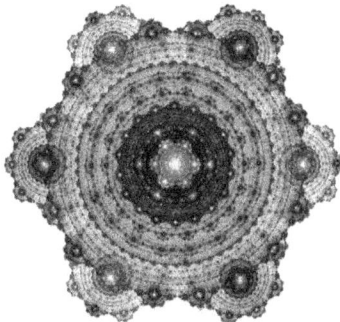

Big Break

A mask came by and rang my bell
And told me I had won the prize
Opened the door and oh how I fell
For the impeccable disguise

I beheld all the elements of a face
A pair of beady myopic eyes
Casting that perfect pose of grace
Lips dripping with delicious lies
Under a nose that never tasted a rose
But had bouquets all over the place

Best to break even
On those big breaks
'Cause the bigger the tent
The bigger the stakes
On the fast-track to a cul-de-sac
Riding a jacked-up Cadillac
Take care your big break
Doesn't break you right back
Yeah, be sure your big break
Doesn't break you right back

Opportunity knockin' knockin'
Or at least that's how it sounds
Opportunity knockin' knockin'
Knock you flat down on the ground

Promenade of prominence
Doin' the dirty dance of dissonance
Half an inch away from success
And thirsty as Tantalus

Hotshot used-song salesman
Really knew how to work the lot
Turn a junkyard into a caravan
And a rowboat into a yacht

Discord rode up on a shiny pony
Oozing tons of I don't know what
Her perfume smelled like alimony
Eyes like a knife to the gut

They rode off into the sunset
Leaving a trail of broken hearts
A shadow and a silhouette
Off to one hell of a start

Incredible

Diogenes went a-hunting for an honest man
Said I'll surely find one if I can
I've been all up and down this land
But I've never seen the real deal first-hand

All of the balance and none of the check
It's about as fair as you might expect
Cork popping on the bottleneck
Dealing from the bottom of half-stacked decks

Northbound suddenly heading south
Two truths coming from a single mouth
Didn't know the world was so flexible
It's absolutely incredible

I carry a lamp by the broad light of day
Ever seeking new ways to disobey
Heckling authority is my true forte
Scraping by on panhandler's pay

I've heard words that beggar belief
Raised in defense of a millionaire thief
Hiding behind a little fig leaf
But a two-bit hustler gets no relief

I've been to bordellos and boardrooms
I've seen manure spruced with perfume
Watched while wolves pull on wool costumes
Cozying up the sheep they're about to consume

Northbound suddenly heading south
Two truths coming from a single mouth
Didn't know the world was so flexible
It's absolutely incredible

Non Sequitur

Yo-yo
Pogo stick
Wax and wick
Icy slick logistic tricks
Concrete streets
Crack my feet
Up and down
Smile and frown
Whichever verb does the noun

Knick-knacks
Triple stacked
Take up slack
Whacking at the hacky-sack
Kicking air
Nothing there
In and out
Faith and doubt
Whatever this is all about

Tick-tock
Kick the clock
Round the block
Groovin' on gridlock
Non sequitur
Are you sure?
Now and then
Who and when
Better confiscate their pens

Yin yang
Finger bang
Sir you rang
Hierarchical harangue
Jump how high?
Scrape the sky
Go and stay
Night and day
Planetary plug and play

Jumpin' jackhammer
Slip the slammer
Grimoire grammar
Late and great
Out-wait and activate
Correlate unrelated dates
Scrambled boggle
Moon boondoggles
Infra-violet goggles
Helmet meet baton
Hamster marathon
Let's immanentize an Eschaton

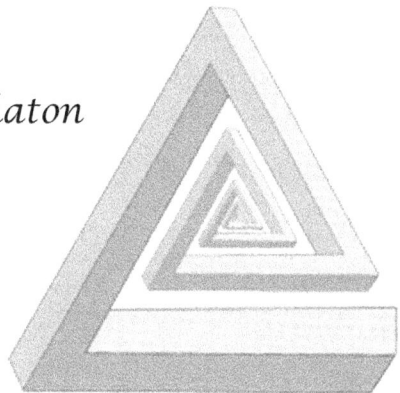

Raincheck

It all began innocently enough
Like an out-of-hand poker bluff
Improvising ad-libbed alibis
Losing track of the runaway lies

Little white slips of omission
Piling in a tinderbox awaiting ignition
Making way for stray flames bound
To torch our totems down to the ground

It may seem an abdication
A way to duck an altercation
I owe a ton of explanations
But it's too sunny for a spat
So you'll have to take a raincheck on that

There was a clear intention
For some well-timed mention
When the mere revelation
Won't trigger Armageddon

Painted into a corner
Of shady evasive maneuvers
No broad brush is gonna cover
The graffiti left by other lovers

It may seem an abdication
A way to duck an altercation
I owe a ton of explanations
But it's too sunny for a spat
So you'll have to take a raincheck on that

I know I'm pissing in the potion
Playing with everyone's emotions
Yeah, I've set some things in motion
That are bound to cause a commotion

Three sides to every triangle
But only one end to this tangle
Slice this Gordian cord to ribbons
So we can all get on with being forgiven

It may seem an abdication
A way to duck an altercation
I owe a ton of explanations
But it's too sunny for a spat
So you'll have to take a raincheck on that

Playing On Principles

I say, who let the nest egg loose?
What's good for the golden goose
Is good for another excuse
Predictable predicaments
And bottomless problems
Chances misspent
As we scramble for ransom

Maybe we'll strike platinum
Or at least some silver shekels
Fortune's a pendulum
Hitting the pits and the pinnacles
They call it a windfall
Cause wealth is ephemeral

Oh we're gonna make it rain
We're gonna make it flood
So better get up on the high ground
Or be knee-deep in the mud
If you'll trade your soul for treasure
You've got a solid claim on neither

I came to this game
With my naivete intact
I don't care to spend my rhythm
Trying to watch my back
Mighty generous with my trust
Not because I can, but because I must

Oh we're gonna make it rain
We're gonna make it flood
So better get up on the high ground
Or be knee-deep in the mud
If you'll trade your soul for treasure
You've got a solid claim on neither

Pocket full of intangibles
Guessin' hard and playing on principles
Gamblin' big on little symbols
However the cards might shuffle
The real jackpot belongs
To those who hang on all night long
For the sake of the song
For the sake of the song

Bullet Points

I see your pride is well-fortified
As serious as cyanide
Circles of self-justified
Splitting hairs till they won't divide
I'm not tryin' to sound too snide
But what you've denied wasn't even implied

Your points strike me a little hollow
As I'm sure you already know
An awful lot of lead to swallow
Your shots are aiming low
And somehow I can't quite follow
Where exactly you expect this to go

Showed up for a showdown
Armed to the eyeballs
Waging your one-man war
But I sure ain't the Sheriff
You should be gunnin' for
No, I ain't the Sheriff
You should be gunnin' for

I see you brought both big guns
Double-barreled jargon
Plenty of loaded questions
And explosive ammunition
But I didn't come to duel at dawn
The hour is early and day is young

Since we're both being candid
And sparring backhanded
I really think the ego has landed
Your senses have left you stranded
But my hands are up as you commanded
And I've been duly reprimanded

Showed up for a showdown
Armed to the eyeballs
Waging your one-man war
But I sure ain't the Sheriff
You should be gunnin' for
No, I ain't the Sheriff
You should be gunnin' for

With your leave, I'll take my exit
Truth is yet the moving target
No golden hammers or silver bullets
Are really gonna be able to nail it
There's phantoms in our blankets
And elephants in the closet

Sailing In Circles

Ah, those were our halcyon nights
Dancing on fantasy's ledge
Outlandish pied-piper satellites
Pushing the envelope over the edge

The stars all shining spectral rays
And the ocean was but a lake
Sailing in circles for a thousand days
Swept away as we fell awake

Oh, all of us felt the loss
From the four-way double-cross
When the arrow hit the albatross
And the headless coin was tossed
First it soars and then it tumbles
Well, that's the way the karma crumbles

Captain took a turn for the strange
Missing the storm-clouds for the sea
Icebergs high as a mountain range
Rumbling whispers of mutiny

The vessel sank like stoneware
In wells of washed-out ink
Wisdom, wisdom everywhere
But not a thought to think

Oh, all of us felt the loss
From the four-way double-cross
When the arrow hit the albatross
And the headless coin was tossed
First it soars and then it tumbles
Well, that's the way the karma crumbles

Gotta get it off my chest
My chest
Oh I gotta get it off my chest
My chest

The sightless prophet held his head
Salty and parched with thirst
Bring that bird back from the dead
And your fate shall be reversed

If your raft survives resurrection
And rises up from the murky deep
Casting a still life reflection
Of when dreams were only asleep

Slums of Columbia

With Flash Mountain Flood
First performed 5/21/15

On the road to what I'd become
Hypnotized by the highway hum
I spotted a wild young bum
Stickin' out his thumb
Unwashed and underfed
Holding a sign that read
"Will Work For Play"
It's a pretty fair deal
When you put it that way

It takes one to know one
And we were running out of sun
So I said hop in, but you may as well know
My blood runs pure hobo
And I live life on the go
My elders rode the rails
Living large on songs and tall tales
Worked the system from the outside lookin' in
'Cause there was no work to be had within

Bummed out in the slums of Columbia
Aimlessly chasing crumbs
Swimming in rivers of rum
A little wisdom's always welcome
Well, I'll tell you where you're heading
If you'll show me where you're coming from

Oh, y'know ole Captain Kirk
He was in it for the perks
In his back alley office hard at work
Emptying bottles behind the Blue Note Bar
Gettin' rid of the leftover liquor
And Stretch wrecked his leg, but not in the war
No, he got bit by an angry railroad car
Ole Lyin' Charlie with that razzle-dazzle charm
Never let truth stand in the way of a yarn

Bummed out in the slums of Columbia
Aimlessly chasing crumbs
Swimming in rivers of rum
A little wisdom's always welcome
Well, I'll tell you where you're heading
If you'll show me where you're coming from

We went round and round
And wound up back at the same old town
Life's pretty simple when you strip it down
All you have for sale's a smile
That just might turn someone's day around
And that's how you survive in style
Turn those tears into ragged rhymes
Reminding us that we all
Yeah, all of us feel that way sometimes

Jones

With Flash Mountain Flood

Old man what have you left for us
Fields of poison and cities of rust
The sky painted industrial grey,
Foggin' up tomorrow for your gravy today

Left us nothing but hunger and thirst
That big ole bubble has already burst
Our generation's under a mountain of debt
The only part of school we won't soon forget

Show us the carrot show us the stick
You better go ahead and take your pick
Whether it's a cubicle or holding cell
There's a place for you at the Jones' Motel

Strung out on flesh and bones
Hung up by that naggin' Jones
Some are stuck with needles
Others the arrow of love
Even the flowers are hooked
On sunshine raining from above

What is this place where have we gone?
There's a cold breeze and an empty dawn
They say you can count on taxes and death
Soon they'll tax your very breath

Jones got us grinding our lives away
But today's worth more than the factory pays
My guitar always has this deep urge to play
Jonesin' for more strummin' every day

We're hooked on water, hooked on air
Hooked on each other, I do declare
All these Joneses you'd better feed
If you can tell a want from a need

Strung out on flesh and bones
Hung up by that naggin' Jones
Some are stuck with needles
Others the arrow of love
Even the flowers are hooked
On sunshine raining from above

Elysium

Went out tilting at windmills
Across groundless molehills
Tried to hitch a ride to the spectacle
Hangin' on to the edge of my skull

And my thumb went numb
Waiting for the answer to come
So I asked the travelers at random
If they knew the way to Elysium
If they knew the way to Elysium

The paradox of paradise
Heaven's only a slice
Without the underworld's fire
The whole globe would be on ice

One broke out his flowchart
Elegant with gold-inlaid art
Said depends on where you start
Destiny has got a lot of moving parts

The next said I know but will not tell
But what if we sit here for a spell
Upon this unhinged carousel
And reflect our paths in parallel
Reflect our paths in parallel

The paradox of paradise
Heaven's only a slice
Without the underworld's fire
The whole globe would be on ice

For a while we spun all the dials
And turned that inch into many miles
Still I remained an empty exile
Chasing the impossible endless smile

I built a scenic bridge to forever
Whiled away ages in the endeavor
Stranger said, well, that's very clever
But you're gonna need a bigger lever
Yeah, you're gonna need a bigger lever

Moment of Zen

Wakin' up touchy and cranky
Tryin' to shake my own skin
Feels so terribly itchy
And unbearably thin
Must be some kind of allergy
Or just reality kicking in

It'll be quite a confession
But I won't call it a sin
I'm just not who I was back then
I'm not sorry that it happened
Only about when
It wasn't my intention
But I'd do it all over again

There's no time like the present
To have that talk about the future
No time like the present
To put those dreams out to pasture
Here it is, my moment of Zen
Pluck my lucky clover and count to ten
Then waltz right into the lion's den
And hope that we can still be friends

My ripped trousers need some mending
Never mind the fences I'm straddling
Disaster perpetually pending
And the close calls are never ending
But the dreaded deadline keeps extending

The orchard's a secret for tranquility's sake
But the fruit looks ripe and ready to shake
We've reached the point of bend or break
See how much rattling this house can take
At the epicenter of a full-blown truth-quake

Delivering last year's news
Headline unread and printed in blues
And that ticking time-bomb can't be defused
I wish you'd just read the ten-foot clues
But we all live in the illusions we choose

The words that weigh ten thousand pounds
If I could only make myself make the sounds
For this one might bring the house down
Better turn you on to what's going around
Before it becomes the talk of the town

The Judge's Daughter

There was a cruel judge who dealt in dread
Sentencing the living to join the dead
He decreed an annual Athenian feast
Be fed to an unspeakable bull-headed beast
Sacrificed in a cavernous maze
To meet the monster at the end of their days

The judge had a few troubles at home
Namely a wife who was prone to roam
Short on mercy and quick with the hammer
And then there was this prince in his slammer
Who on the eve of slaughter
Stole the love of the Judge's daughter

With your feet dipped in fire
Running free your sole desire
When you've caught the heat
And it can't get any hotter
Just don't burn
The Judge's daughter

Ariadne, she was a firebrand ready to flee
Said oh, lover, I'll set you free,
But only if you swear to bring me
If I stay, why, I'll lose my head
So track the way with this thread
And out of the labyrinth you'll be led

Been thinking since you first arrived
That I might prefer you make it alive
Stick with me and you'll survive
This court is rife with sorrow and strife
So please just take me and make me your wife
I've danced in this dungeon all my life

With your feet dipped in fire
Running free your sole desire
When you've caught the heat
And it can't get any hotter
Just don't burn
The Judge's daughter

A steep price now upon their heads
The fugitive lovers quickly fled
Bats out of Hades' realm of the dead
Now he was a prisoner of love instead
One night they made it on moonlit sands
As she slept he made other plans

Ariadne saw she'd been played like a pawn
He'd gone and left her by the early dawn
You'd think with love so tough to find
Such sweetness wouldn't be left behind
But heroes hate to get tied down
With beauties waiting in every town

Psilly

Boom boom boom
Magical mushroom
Boom boom boom
Magical mushroom
Wow wow wow
Holy cow!
Wow wow wow
Holy cow!

Gonna stick my head in a golden cap
Lay down and melt all the maps
While primordial thunderclaps
Wonder if the world's ready to snap

Among the dung some monkeys know
The shimmering silver mushrooms grow
Every where the cattle go
They leave a trail to follow

Stoned ape feelin' psilly
Picking out the prize
There's a whole new horizon
Poppin' in those pies

Spores from before the human race
Some say they hail from outer space
In any case an interface
Way beyond the commonplace

Out in grassy pastures
Nature speaks in pictures
Telescoping textures
And auditory architecture

Stoned ape feelin' psilly
Picking out the prize
There's a whole new horizon
Poppin' in those pies

Boom boom boom
Magical mushroom
Boom boom boom
Magical mushroom
Wow wow wow
Holy cow!
Wow wow wow
Holy cow!

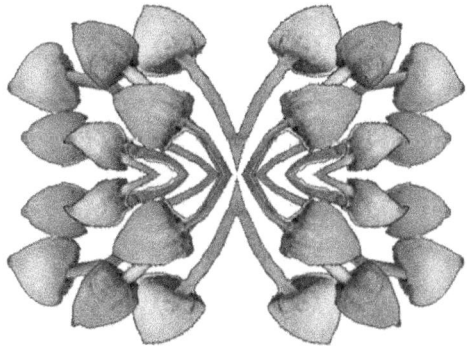

Mess of Lentils

It was the night that someday came
The moon blossomed and I did the same
Miracles in a circle bearing my name
Purple sage said go now stake your claim
And never forsake it for wealth or fame

Called forth the birthright on my knees
A floating bright light beckoning me
Rippling in an unseen breeze
A whisper urging me to seize
The thread of the Dead with delicate ease

The snag's quite a drag
But the balloon hasn't popped
We weren't brought this way just to get stopped
We didn't fly the night sky only to be dropped
Perched on the precipice, one and all
And we didn't come this far
Only to fall

Follow that voice and be well led
If you dare tread raging riverbeds
Let resonant words be heard and said
But don't you trade it for an inflated head
A red mess of lentils or thin slice of bread

Heirloom treasure one can't keep
Conferring pleasure doesn't come cheap
You'd better be ready to dig real deep
Fail and flail and wail and weep
Measure by measure on a groundless leap

The snag's quite a drag
But the balloon hasn't popped
We weren't brought this way just to get stopped
We didn't fly the night sky only to be dropped
Perched on the precipice, one and all
And we didn't come this far
Only to fall

The waking dream came and went
Throughout the winters of discontent
Twisted forks mentally bent
Mixed messages hastily sent
And who knew what any of it meant

Mondegreen Stew

There's more here than meets the ear
More than anyone understands
Like an old story told fourth hand
The only constant is conversion
Everyone hears a different version
Pass it on, pass a ton
Past a one, past we won

There was an out-of-the-way café
So I wandered right on in
At once the audio buffet
Triggered a sense of recognition
I was offered a selection
Of sweet admonitions
Served with hot-cross puns
And double-shots of expression

There were troubadours in the rear
In the midst of an open-mike session
A parade of more or lessons
Misbegotten ballads
In rapid succession
Tossed word salads
Litanies of confession
And sea-soaked shanties of salty insurrection

It's the Universe at the end of the restaurant
Where food for thought is easily bought
And chaos ordered anew
Serving misheard Mondegreen stew
Battered earslips and eggcorns to dip
With a side of mangled malaprops too

This one sings farewell lull-a-byes
And we all shed a tear and sigh
That one slings barbed lampoons
Slick and dripping with crude
This one came with steam to vent
Scalding with bristling rage
Squeezed between broken laments
Mourning the darkness of our age

This one grumbles gritty blues
Woe woe woe a world of bad news
That one wails tales of mutinies
Betrayals by bygone buccaneers
Someone hails victories
Trumpeted in yesterday's lore
Someone thunders the wonder
Of tomorrow's rising roar

Tributary

Never mind me, I've got an eight-track mind
The kind that isn't built to ever rewind
Fast forward, fast forward
In the current there's only one way to go
Toward the future as the river flows

Just a channel of a tributary
And you can call me anything but lazy
Rushing rapids, rushing rapids
Mountains stand still, but I'm in a hurry
And probably will be for eternity

Panning sentiments
For whatever seems to glow
Toes buried in sediment
Knee-deep in indigo
Always an experiment
In the riverflow

A river lives between the lines
Filling in the Earth's cracked design
Drink deeply, think deeply
The papyrus reeds hieroglyphic signs
Where ancient ideas remain enshrined

I say my way is the high way
Never yet has led me astray
Washing away, washing away
The dirt of many derelict days
Clinging on to crusty feet of clay

You'll find I don't mind heading downhill
Inclined to bend toward gravity's will
Everyone loves to watch a waterfall
Sloppy and wet, it's my nature to spill
Wherever there's a fault to fill

The stream is a creature of reflection
Knowing only its own direction
Following the golden hollow
Oozing from the pores of conception
In search of the perfect imperfection

Panning sentiments
For whatever seems to glow
Toes buried in sediment
Knee-deep in indigo
Always an experiment
In the riverflow

Folio

If there's one takeaway from Shakespeare
It's that we're all going though a stage
And that the play will be less unclear
If everyone cues off the same page

We're led by a reluctant director
And the script's chock full of holes
With a cast and crew of bad actors
Entirely unfit for their roles

Folded in faded folios
Whether famous or infamous
Too late to stay anonymous
We are never born to greatness
No, greatness must be thrust upon us

My reputation seems to proceed me
And it is surely bound to follow
So spare me your vicarious vanity
The chants of sycophants echo hollow

I am what iamb, and that is all I am
A soliloquy of errors
Some lines to get you out of a jam
And hold your soul up to a mirror

Folded in faded folios
Whether famous or infamous
Too late to stay anonymous
We are never born to greatness
No, greatness must be thrust upon us

Dressed in the drama of our portrayals
Mighty easy to forget who you are
Tangled in all the layers of veils
The costumes worn by unlit stars

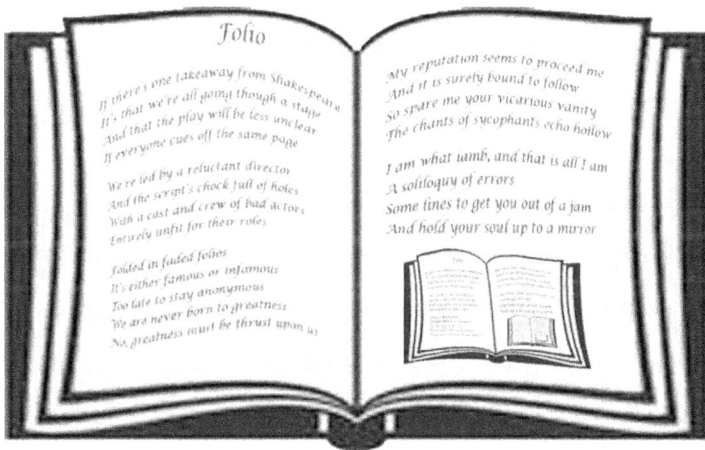

Folio

If there's one takeaway from Shakespeare
It's that we're all going though a stage
And that the play will be less unclear
If everyone cues off the same page

We're led by a reluctant director
And the script's chock full of holes
With a cast and crew of bad actors
Entirely unfit for their roles

folded in faded folios
It's either famous or infamous
Too late to stay anonymous
We are never born to greatness
No, greatness must be thrust upon us

My reputation seems to proceed me
And it is surely bound to follow
So spare me your vicarious vanity
The chants of sycophants echo hollow

I am what I am, and that is all I am
A soliloquy of errors
Some lines to get you out of a jam
And hold your soul up to a mirror

Pigeonhole

Because you've seen a side of me
You might think you've seen it all
Relegate me to the role you see
As if anyone were that small

I'm often confused with my depiction
It's a case of mistaken identity
Yes, sir, I do fit the description
But no, that doesn't begin to cover me

It'll take one hell of a spell
To pull out of that gravity well
What's the escape velocity for a soul
Caught in a mile-deep pigeonhole?

Typecast, all too suitable for the part
So much the world takes it to heart
And all you want is to get on with the art
But the preconceptions won't let you start

Showman trading shades of shamans
Doves are just privileged pigeons
And everybody loves a good magician
Whatever you choose to call your musicians

The method channels manifestation
Consumed by character's motivation
Been known to embody an emulation
But I'm more than the sum of your expectations

It'll take one hell of a spell
To pull out of that gravity well
What's the escape velocity for a soul
Caught in a mile-deep pigeonhole?

What can I say, it fit me like a glove
As if cast by some playwright above
To show us all that push come to shove
They're all doves if you show enough love

That's the way the rumors roll
I wouldn't touch them with a ten-foot pole
How you see me is beyond my control
But I won't stay stuck in a pigeonhole

Aftermyth

Held a coronation for a scarecrow
Crowned by a setting-sun halo
Planted lines of wind in sterile soil
Watered with essential oils
Come summer still tilling a field of dust
Just us and that straw-boss
Out of time and out of trust

The dream's still real
It's reality that's fake
And another dream unravels
Every time I wake
A lot of baggage to travel with
But we'll outlive the Aftermyth

We spoke the unspeakable out loud
Danced up a storm among the clouds
Split the sky and kicked loose rain
Trickling down in liquid refrains
And the beanstalks sprouted tall and thin
But crafty Jack did the giant in
For a flimsy sack of gilded tin

The dream's still real
It's reality that's fake
And another dream unravels
Every time I wake
A lot of baggage to travel with
But we'll outlive the Aftermyth

We're way past the very last straw
There's no un-seeing the things we saw
The masks are off on faces of clay
All too clear by stark naked day
Oh, there it goes, on a single wing
Caught in a vortex of reckoning
Tangled up in intricate not-work strings

Now What?

Now what what now?
And who and where and when and how
The skyscape grey and thick with wonder
Dripping silver rain and golden thunder
Who now will color the numbers with notes
Who now will paint the dawn with immortal quotes
What will blossom in the wake of the dead
After planting a chip of ice-nine in your head
But that lost ship has long since sailed
And that train of thought has been derailed

Now we'd best figure out some future
As skeletons assume
Room temperature
Well, the unknown remains no less vast
But at least we can dance away the past

Let us carve our names in the feast
From the loftiest to the very least
Raise empty cups in a booming toast
Weep and fill ballrooms with empty boasts
Who would dare to stand on ceremony
Sipping wine flavored with ashes and acrimony
As the phantoms rise up to speak
Howling, haunting, ghostly tongues in cheek
Better put your actions where your notions are
Or this spaceship's not going to get very far

Now's a phase we're zipping through
Here's a space which follows you
I tell you, they knew the brew
A dash of old and splash of new
Something borrowed and something true
It's all smoke and mirrors from the fan's-eye view
But it's still crystal clear from the fan's-eye view

Now we pony up and play
Lay down an ace a deuce or a trey
Wild multitudes milling and scattered
As another fragile fantasyland shatters
Look at the armies of schism a-risin'
Numinous clouds looming off the horizon
Stumbling and rumbling toward resurrection
A thousand heads casting in every direction
Chasing rainbows and hunting untold gold
Hidden in folds a half-century old

Now we'd best figure out some future
As skeletons assume
Room temperature
Well, the unknown remains no less vast
But at least we can dance away the past

Unasked

For the Good Doctor

Now, let's hear it
What does silence say?
How do phantoms pass the day?
How much does a dream weigh
After doubt has chased it away?
What random tangent shall we entertain?
These are the pressing questions
Unasked in their very expression

What a heavy day in the laboratory
We've set off in uncharted territory
Let's see if we can levitate gravity
Or sort static from synchronicity
Not nearly as noble as dynamite
And darker than stars devouring their own light
Bellowing every now and then fire-demons of spite
Scorching the source of all we ignite

Here we've visited vistas
Of unintelligible synesthesia
Here Mnemosyne wrestles perpetually
With her evil twin Amnesia

Here have we overflown lands
Overgrown by phoney panaceas
Here we scaled loops of circular stairs
And plunging neckline nadirs of despair
As we distilled volatile emotions
Into smokey lyrical potions
Ideas getting carried away with themselves
Born to greatness but bound to bookshelves
It's all very quick and terribly clever
But where shall we find the wizard healer
Who knows how to cure the broken lover?

Let us consider the cost of consideration
The drag of deliberation
As we design experiments
Destined to end in conflagration
And attempt to invent acrobatic instruments
Intent on self-examination
Without bending them and sending them
Into maddened luminous hyperspheres
Blinded by the navel's glorious glare
These are the pressing questions
Unasked in their very expression

Is there a real difference between forgery and art?
Does it matter if the buyer can't tell them apart?
Is the culture past the date of expiration
Spoiled with murky curdled traditions
Devoid of any credible claim
To serving any reasonable aim
Or can one cull a strain of redemption
Immune to the pangs of conception
Is there any sense assigning blame
When cure and poison are exactly the same?

What are gods made in the image of?
Is time truly a Titan
Which swallows its children
All the while protesting love?
Thundering conflicting commands
From lofty mountaintops above
As the faithful cut off their own hands
Fearful to trust their own plans
These are the pressing questions
Unasked in their very expression

Will ideals keep caving to expediency?
What would it even mean to be completely free?
Where's the hope for anarchy
When some warlord half-cocked big shot
Marauding with an unopposed army
Directly erects another dynasty?

After all, if the Empire were to fall
How many of us would survive at all?
These are the pressing questions
Unasked in their very expression

How does one plot out
The origin of originality?
What came before eternity?
When did these broken notions of sin
Get twisted and mixed in
With evoking inner divinity?
How do we swallow our own tales
Taken to compass the cosmic scale?

Usual suspects rounded up and released
All the props of philosophers and priests
Yet the mystery of ontology remains unsolved
And now the lab has utterly dissolved
Who cares who did it
We want to know why
Even if we only find plausible lies
All the mind's cages buckled and bent
No one knows where the control group went
Medals all melted down again
Has the entire universe fallen in
Collapsing all which might have been?
These are the pressing questions
Unasked in their very expression

Notable Quotables
ASAOS

"Analogy is the screwdriver in a writer's toolbox."

"The more you learn about literature, the less you want to be a writer."

"Will work for play."

"Only a damn Fool expects a poet to be a perfect person. After all, you don't get to be a poet without making some pretty poor choices."

"That's the way the karma crumbles..."

"Artists shouldn't cater to the tastes of the audience. Artists are the caterers of taste."

"Love is magical. Ignore it, and it vanishes."

"Polyamory may not be unilaterally declared."

"Excuses are the refuge of those who fear it might be safer to fail."

"The simplest statements are the most elusive."

"My three favorite precious metals: Fool's Gold, Liquid Silver, and Stainless Irony."

"Just because you're narcissistic doesn't mean you aren't fabulous..."

"The first-person point of view seems to me to be the only authentic perspective. All else is hearsay."

"The Great Work is all about getting Over your Self."

"The faith of a Fool is the most powerful force in human nature."

"I firmly believe in agnosticism."

"Never underestimate the power of ghosts. We ourselves are living phantoms, stretching out through time, fleeting and eternal."

"I've been hearing disturbing rumors lately about my mental health and I'd like to put all concerns to rest. I am pleased to report that I'm mad as ever, probably more so, with no signs of sanity in sight."

More lyric verse
by Indi Riverflow:
Gyroscape

Contact: ampi@amanamission.com

Rhapsody In Retrograde

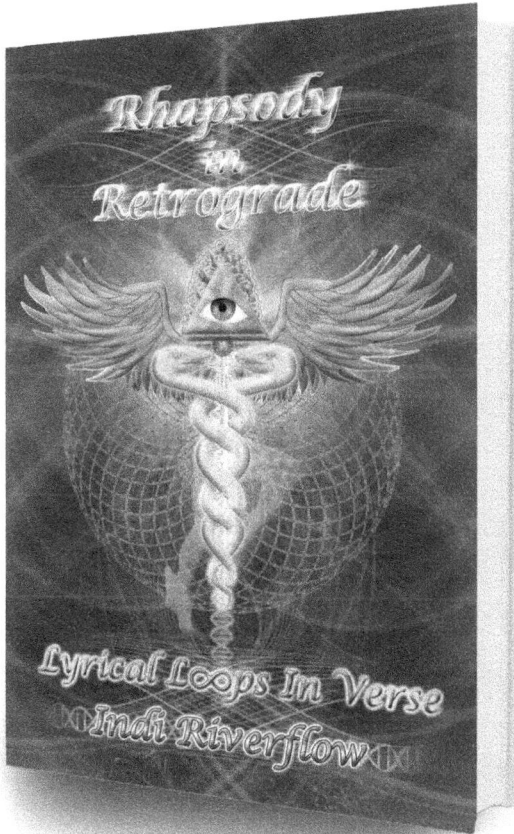

Amana Mission Publishing Ink
Alternative Press

To Incite Insight
www.amanamission.com

www.ingramcontent.com/pod-product-compliance
Lightning Source LLC
Chambersburg PA
CBHW020913090426
42736CB00008B/605